Experiencing

The Present

of

GOD'S

PRESENCE

Julie B Cosgrove

Experiencing the Present of His Presence
Short Reflections to help you find God in your day

Printed in the United States of America
Cross Word Press, Fort Worth, TX
ISBN: (p) 978-1-329-43687-9

Dedicated to my sister Anne, Linda,
and to
all of you who so encourage me
with your frequent blog comments.

Table of Contents

Forward

Have you seen evidence of God in your life recently?

God often revealed Himself through signs and wonders throughout the Bible, and I believe He still does so today. His holiness breaks through the mundane and transforms it to get our attention—like a celestial shoulder tap telling us He loves us, wishes to correct our path, wants to instruct us, or let us know He's still here watching over us. I call this action the present of His presence.

Perhaps most of us will never have a burning bush experience, but that doesn't mean there isn't evidence of our Lord's desire to be a part of our lives. Most likely, you've had suck-in-breath incidents in your past when a holy chill zipped up your arms as you realized you'd just experienced a "God moment." Maybe a sentence in a sermon or a lyrical line in a hymn brought a tear to your eye. It might have been a verse in Scripture that you'd never noticed before, and for a split-second pondered if God had penned it for you in that moment in time. Possibly someone, even a child, pierced your heart with their wisdom.

For me, God speaks a great deal through His creation. Growing up, I spent much of my summers at our extended family's cabin in the Texas Hill Country. While Mom fixed breakfast, Dad took us for nature hikes in the cool of the mornings. He'd point out insects under leaves, cloud formations and bird calls. To this day I often notice things that rarely catch another's eye—a bird pecking for its lunch in a tree trunk, an industrious ant carrying three times its weight on the sidewalk while in danger of being crushed by human feet, or a cloud formation that resembles, well...whatever.

God meets us where we are and through our experiences in life. He speaks to us in a spiritual language often times only meant for our faith-ears. He demonstrates His omnipotence during our day to draw our faith-eyes to His presence. This is a special gift of love for us and us alone. Perhaps as an answer to prayer, or a wake-up call, or simply a reassurance He cares for whatever we happen to be going through at the time.

However personal and special these fleeting moments in the presence of holiness are, I believe they are meant to be shared in order to witness to His love and to bolster others to seek Him in their day as well. When told I should have a blog because I am an author and devotional writer, I questioned why the world needed another Christian one? After much prayer, which involved a lot of listening, God revealed to me that the main underlining theme in all my writing— be it fiction or non-fiction—involved helping people discover Him in their lives. Thus, in the fall of 2011, my blog *Where Did You Find God Today* came into existence.

I told God—yes, bold of me I know—that if I developed this He'd have to specifically bop me over the head with ideas as to what I should write. He has been faithful to do that, and because of this, my faith has deepened beyond measure. I began this blog at a time of transition in my life as a new widow, and knowing God cared enough to reveal Himself to me and then entrust me with recording it as an inspiration to others has often brought me to my knees in humble awe.

So often in our scurrying through the busyness of life, we don't truly observe what happens around us. Our "to-do" lists become spiritual blinders, which tend to narrow our perspective. It is my prayer that, by reading these postings off and on during your quiet time, some will help spawn ways you can detect our Lord moving in your day, each and every day, whether in a burning bush or something a bit more ordinary.

His presence is a special present wrapped up and tied with a bow. He has written your name on the tag. Now, open it and smile. See, it's just what you needed.

Seek Him in His righteousness first and foremost, and soon everything else will fall into proper perspective. (Matthew 6:33 paraphrased.)

Julie B Cosgrove
www.juliebcosgrove.com
http://wheredidyoufindgodtoday.com

NOTE:

At the end of each lesson are opportunities to discuss a few questions. This is intended for a group, however, you may also use them to help guide your personal journeying.

Whether you use the discussion suggestions or not, I hope these short reflections encourage you to seek Him in your day as He so often has done so in mine.

Two Letters, Two Ways

Hi, my name is Julie and I am a word-aholic. I play Scrabble with the computer, and have at least fifteen Words with Friends (WWF) games going at once. On my smart phone are four other solitary word games to keep me occupied while I am waiting for my friends to send me their word entries. This morning as i sipped my coffee, after my prayer and devotional time of course, I had a few minutes to play a few of the WWF puzzles. Starting a rematch, this is what popped up in my tile selection: T ? U I E N S

At first, this word popped into my head, so I played it. Yes, I didn't use the blank. (A strategic move on my part, heh, heh.)

But I realized, another word could be spelled with the very same letters simply by flipping the letter "I" and the letter "T". UNTIES can become UNITES.

It brought to mind Jesus' words to Peter when he told him his name would now be Cephas, the Rock on which He'd build his Church.

> *...whatever you bind on earth will be bound in heaven, and whatever you loose on earth will be loosed in heaven.* Matthew 16:19b

That has been passed on to all Christians in the Great Commission. We have two choices with the times, talents and treasures God had provided us. We can use them to untie ourselves from others, i.e separate us from them. We can strive for the bigger house, better car, more toys, and more expensive vacays. We can also use our God-given talents to shine the light of pride on whatever we do, thus distinguishing us from the crowd. We untie (loose) the ropes that binds us to others so we can be set apart as better, stronger, smarter...

Or, we can use our God-given abilities to unite (bind) ourselves to others. Through loving God, and serving Him as an expression of that love, we act as a binding force to draw others into the fold. Bound together in His goodness and mercy, we are strengthened, supported, and secured. That's the servitude attitude Jesus displayed while on earth.

God gives us the letters to play. It up to us to determine how we use the "I" (me) and the "T"(them).

DISCUSS:

What happens when we put others first instead ourselves.

Should we always place others' considerations and needs before our own?

When should we not?

Clearly

 I saw a picture of a glass of water. Pure, thirst quenching, clear.

Water is something we need to survive. We can't go very long without it. Our bodies have water running through them. No wonder Jesus told the Samaritan woman at the well in midday He is the Living Water.

> Jesus answered her, "If you knew the gift of God and who it is that asks you for a drink, you would have asked him and he would have given you *living water*." John 4:10

God's blessings overflow, providing us what we need to make it through the day. But, like a glass of water, sometimes we can see right through them, and so we don't really "see." Or what we see is distorted by the container, i.e. us.

Other times we want to add something to the water to make it taste better. Sugar, lemons, mint, cucumbers, even those small packets of energy-booster flavorings are added. We brew coffee through it, or steep tea in it. We add seltzer and make it bubbly. But your doctor will tell you there is nothing better for you than a plain, pure glass of water. In fact, most Americans are chronically dehydrated and don't realize it. We swallow everything but pure water in order to quench our thirst.

The same is true with God's blessings. Too many of us try to satisfy our "thirst" with other things than Christ. I plead guilty.

Yet He is the one thing we need to make it through. Receive Him, drink Him down and quench your soul.
Have I made you thirsty? I pray God makes you thirst for more of Him today. Drink in His blessings. Clearly, they will be there if you look. Gulp them down and say, "ahhh."

DISCUSS:

Health scientists say we need to drink about a half gallon per day, which can include water based beverages (as long as they are not more than 40% of your total consumption.) Do you drink enough water each day? Why or why not?

Some people today are obsessed with water consumption and thus suffer from water intoxication and possible hypnoatermia. Can we become too obsessed with God?

Illuminated

I saw an advertisement for glow-in-the-dark paint which you can apply to a stone path.

AHA! Reminds me of the Word of God.

> *Thy word is a lamp unto my feet, and a light unto my path.* Psalm 119:105

The ad says the chemicals absorb the sunlight, so when it becomes dark, they release a glow. That way, people can see the way to travel and not stumble. This miracle paint is for sale at most of the national hardware chain stores.

While my life is sunny and things are going great, I should be storing up passages from God's Word and memorizing them. Let them ooze into my heart and soul just as the glow-in-the-dark paint seeps into the porous stone.

The Word of God should illuminate my faith so when the dark times come, and they will, I will have them stored up inside of me. One by one, the faith-stones will light my way along the path, even though I cannot see where it leads. Then, instead of crouching and crying out in fear, afraid I may stumble, I can walk upright, assured that God's light will guide me through.

Are you storing up His Light in you? You can get it at any local book store, or as a free app on your smart phone. It is called the Bible. Illuminating, right?

DISCUSS:

When was the last time you felt surrounded by darkness and then found a God-given light across your path?

What are various ways God lights our path and guide us?

Have you ever been the light of Christ shining in someone else's darkness?

It's What's Inside

 An older woman I know excitedly told how she got a part-time job stuffing envelopes. Her eyes danced as if she was a teenager once again. Her nephew questioned what the big deal was. It didn't sound very exciting to him. She smiled. "Oh, it's not the envelopes. It is what goes inside. A very important letter that will help thousands of people. I am so glad to be a part of that effort."

Her words hit me. *It's what goes inside.* The image describes the purpose of being a Christian. We are the vehicle for delivering God's message of redemption and love to the world. In other words, we are the envelopes. It is what is going on inside of us, i.e., the transformation by the Holy Spirit when we accept Jesus into our hearts that is the important stuff. As others peer inside the window to our soul, they can see a difference. Something important is happening. The Light of Christ is flickering, glowing, and then shining. The message revealed is one of forgiveness and salvation, of something more wonderful waiting for us beyond the pain of this world.

Consequently, faith comes from hearing the message, and the message is heard through the word about Christ. Romans 10:17

Lord, the times when I think I am not much on the outside, remind me it is what's inside that is important - You working in me. You have placed your stamp of delivery on me, and I am simply to carry the message. Let me be more thankful, like my elderly friend, to be a part of that effort. Amen.

DISCUSS:

How much emphasis do we put on outwardly appearances? Why do you think that is?

Is it easy to determine what's on the inside of a person, or do you have to get them to open up first?

What keeps others from seeing Christ in us?

Hunger Pains

I was in the zone...typing away, editing as I went, the plot moving along. In the background the washer swished and the dryer tumbled. I'd break to feed a mewing cat, or refill my tumbler with water, and then scoot my chair back to the keyboard before I lost my train of thought.

After a while, a slight wooziness waved over me. I blinked to refocus, only to be interrupted by a deep gurgle in the pit of my torso. Like Seymour, the man eating plant, my stomach growled, "Feed me." I sighed, pushed back my chair and walked to the fridge. Door opened with the frigid air blanketing my face, indecision clouded my brain. I knew not to grab anything junky. I snatched a carton of fat-free Greek yogurt. Quick, easy to down, no cooking or mess to clean. I spooned it past my lips as I typed. That staved off the hunger for a while, but the sensation returned within a few hours.

Isn't this often true of our spiritual lives? We are in such a rush, our concentration focuses on the "doing" mode. We forget that, like our bodies, our souls need regular nourishment in order to function. A deep hunger for God niggles us. At first we ignore it, but it doesn't go away. We know a snack such as a faith based show won't satisfy us. Not even a few Facebook scrolls from Christian friends.

But what to feed it? We flip through a few highlighted verses in our Bibles, scan our bookshelves filled with devotionals and inspirational guides, even stare at the Biblical saying plaques on our walls. We turn on Christian music. Still, the deep aching isn't quite satisfied. We need real God-time. And Sunday is days away.

Regular moments with our Father in Heaven can fulfill us and sustain us as we move through our day. From the half hour spent with hands folded, we receive enough strengthening to carry us through whatever we need to accomplish. Our gas tank refills, so to speak.

In order to fully digest what we read, see and hear, we need to take it to the Father and let His Spirit help us absorb it in order to feed our faith in the way we need the most, just as our bodies assimilate the food we swallow.

Spend quality time with God today. Don't snack now and then as you keep on "doing." Instead, sit down, relax and devour the full-plated goodness God wishes to provide. That's the full meal deal. Talk about soul food!
Blessed are those who hunger and thirst for righteousness, for they will be filled. Matthew 5:6

DISCUSS:
Are you a grazer or do you down a full meal and then wait until you are hungry again? How about in your spiritual life?

Do you ever crave junk food when you know you shouldn't eat it so much? How about your spiritual life?

Cast Your Cares

I stumbled trying to carry a package to my car—down three steps, wrenching my right foot and ankle in the process. In the ER clinic, the nurse dampened a felt covered strip filled with fiberglass and molded it around my foot and calf. Within minutes it had taken a perfect shape, protecting and providing support and strength to my injured extremity. It now fit only me, no one else. Next, he secured it with two stretchy bandages wrapped around and around.

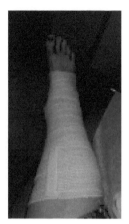

Reminds me of my Savior. Like the fiberglass splint, He is the same for all of us, yet His Spirit molds to me individually, knowing my soul's shape, weaknesses and strengths. He forms a protective shell, guarding my thoughts and shielding me from the evils of this fallen world. All the while He is healing my weaknesses and strengthening me. He guards me from further injury.

Then, similar to the stretchy bandage, His grace and mercy intertwine to further support me, secured by His love. He wraps Himself tightly around my soul when I need it to protect me from further harm.

The doctor told me to not put weight on it for several days, but instead to use crutches. God's Word and blessings are my crutches whenever I fall out of His will. He picks me up, often through the prayers of others, and sets me right.

Having worn a soft cast on my right leg, I've grasped a new meaning of 1Peter 5:7-- *"casting my cares on Him."*

Lord, may I rely on you in my weakness as You strengthen me, and lean on You for support as I heal whenever I tumble from Your grace. Thank You for this valuable lesson, even though painful. Amen.

DISCUSS:

How has the Holy Spirit molded you through the oops, tumbles and stumbles of your life? Are you stronger for it? Give one example.

Though I needed the support, I was glad to occasionally be able to remove the bandages for a bit. Can God's mercy and goodness ever be too confining?

A Quick Cover Up

I had to leave in five minutes. I looked down and gasped. During my showering and hair styling, my nail polish had chipped off on a few nails—ugh!

Now if you aren't a gal, let me explain. This is equivalent to a button popped off or a mustard droplet on a necktie. Not the end of the world, but it definitely screams that you are not put together. Plus, all day you will be self-conscious and imagine everyone is giving you a wide berth and clicking their tongues.

Back to my plight: No time for a manicure. So I dabbed on some more polish to "smooth over" the rough spots. I knew better. With not quite dry nails, I smudged two when I dug in my purse for my car keys. The newly applied coat actually revealed more of the "craters" rather than concealing it. Plus it adhered to the old, making the polish thicker and uneven in places, which made it chip off even more during the day. Now my nails really screamed "Mess!" Sigh.

Well, God used this as a lesson. No, it's not that I have a vanity thing, though there is that I suppose. But how often do we try to cover up our sins thinking the world will not see them? We don't have time to deal with it so we try a quick cover-up. I lost my temper so I will send her flowers. I walked by without saying hello so I will text it later. I took home some copy paper from the office so tomorrow I'll bring brownies. I used the Lord's name in vain so I will put an extra dollar in the offering plate. Quick cover-ups never properly fix the problem.

To set things right, I needed to take the time to remove the old chipped-off stuff, apply a new coat or two of polish and then seal it. Or, at least remove the flaking color and leave my nails fresh and clean. However, that would leave them exposed. Polish and sealant help protect them from breaking. They also add a touch of attractive shine and glimmer.

Couldn't the same be said of my soul? I need to take the time to remove sin by confessing to God, and perhaps another person, the wrong I've done which is chipping away at my relationship. Then I must reapply God's polish-- by reading His Word, colored with prayer and brushed on with a contrite heart--so I can again shine. Lastly, I need to once more be sealed by His merciful Spirit so I am protected. Otherwise, sin will just keep peeling off any attractiveness I present to the world. I will lose my attractiveness.

Whoever conceals their sins does not prosper, but the one who confesses and renounces them finds mercy. Proverbs 28:13

DISCUSS:

Do cover-ups ever really work? Why or why not?

Have you ever tried to conceal something only discover you'd called more attention to it?

Tea Time

Would you think me crazy to say I found God today in my tea cup?

I ADMIT IT. I am an avid Anglophile. (Say that three times fast.) I was weaned on Earl Grey and milk...well, almost. It has always been my comfort drink. When I am hurting, physically or emotionally, just wrapping my fingers around the warm mug and inhaling the soft scent of the tea relaxes me. Then that first creamy sip...hmmm. The world is a better place.

Now, I can drink tea without the cream, but somehow it's not the same. In my opinion, the swirling white liquid changes the color, the texture and enhances the taste. It makes it oh, so much better.

This here is where the God part enters the picture.
My faith acts in much the same way. When I am hurting or frustrated I can wrap my soul around His Spirit. It envelops me and swirls through me. Immediately, I feel as sense of

calm flow over my shoulders and down my back. When, through prayer, I drink in this holy peace, I begin to feels its effects from the inside out.

I suppose I could exist without my faith. Many people do. They drudge through life with a fatalistic, self-orientated attitude. But like the cream in my tea, faith enhances my life. It re-colors it, enriches its flavor, and makes my day more appealing, no matter what happens. I really prefer having that dash of soul-cream in my day. When I pray to my Lord and read His word, it as if I am swirling goodness into my life.

As the tea warms my belly, faith warms my soul.
Of course, there are times I just want to bask in a good cup of tea--just because. Nothing is making me anxious. My aches and pains are minimal. Life is chuggin' along just fine. Get the connection? I knew you would.

Enjoy some tea time with your Lord today.

DISCUSS:

What enriches your life?

What isn't your "cup of tea" that maybe someone else is trying to convince you it should be?

Should everyone spend tea time with God in the same way? Why or why not?

UpRighted

Here in North Texas we are plagued with black beetles. Our cleaning crew at the church can sweep diligently. Yet within hours, the sidewalks and floors are spotted with them again--all on their backs, wiggling their little six legged bodies. (Obviously the bug man's spray works.)

When I first began to work here, my heart bled for these poor bugs that crawled over the invisible poison seeking water and shelter. I hated to see them suffer. So, I would diligently take a leaf or piece of paper and try to flip them over. Maybe if they had enough life left in them flail their legs, they'd be all right if they could just crawl away. But no. Inevitably, the little guys would flip on their backs again and thrash away.

I don't know why God designed them to die on their backs, and I hope they are spared suffering. But, it brought home a valuable lesson. Often, I see others suffering. Many are Christians. They seem to be floundering and are unable to right themselves, just like these beetles. No matter what I do—pray, help, talk—they seems to be stuck in that situation or slump.

I learned God has placed them there for a reason even though I don't know why. It may be to draw them to Him, to diminish their pride, to correct their path... that's between them and God. But I'm confident He never takes His eyes off of them, because when I was flailing on my back, unable to upright myself, I felt my Lord's presence hovering nearby. I heard His whisper, "Hang in there. I'm here."

No matter how hard I try, I simply can't turn my friends upright. But I know the One who can...and will in His own timing if they can just hang in there and keep having faith.
It may happen while they walk on this earth or perhaps one day when they reach Heaven. In the meantime, there is one thing I can do. Pray them through it.

DISCUSS:

Is there someone in your life who is floundering and you don't know how to upright them? What can you do for them and what should you not do?

Will ask others you trust to confidentially pray for them?

If you are unable to upright yourself, will you go to God and if necessary ask a few trustworthy folks to pray over you?

Cat Walk

I live with two cats. One is getting up in year so, he isn't as spry as he once was. Some evenings, I like to veg out on a good Netflix mystery. I sit on my couch with legs stretched to the ottoman. My older  kitty can usually hop up onto the ottoman with effort, but the leap to the couch is more and more beyond his capability. So, smart cat that he is, he has discovered he can use my outstretched legs as a bridge to walk across to my lap.

Jesus died on the cross to bridge the gap between us and God. We now have access to our Father's lap through our Lord and Savior's sacrifice. But we must make the walk, right? We must first take the hop of faith by confessing our sins. Then over Jesus' stretched out arms on the cross, we can come into the Holy presence of our Almighty God. At times it may seem quite an effort, but that's okay. Christ is more than willing to be the conduit that lead us to the throne of grace if we will only make the effort to come to Him first.

For my cat, that first leap onto the ottoman is the hardest part of the journey, but he knows he wants to feel secure and loved in my lap, so it is worth it to him. And when the time comes he is no longer able to hop to the ottoman, my hands will be there to lift him up when he comes to me and meows.

I am no different. I want to feel secured and loved in my Father's presence. Each time I sin, I choose to make that leap of faith in order to ask Christ to be my bridge. Not saying I am as smart as my cat, but I know I am incapable of doing it on my own. I also know I can call on Jesus. He will always be there to lift me up and encourage me to cross over into my Father's lap. He will do the same for you.

DISCUSS:

How hard it is for you to bridge that gap between you and God? Why?

Are there times, even as an adult, you want to crawl into God's lap and be held? Is this being weak? Explain why or why not.

Overload

I felt it coming on. I tried to ignore it, but it kept building. Small things, like my purse dumping all over the floorboard when I turned the corner. Dropping a sack of groceries— not the ones with the eggs, thank the Lord. Catching the pocket of my skirt on the doorknob when my arms were full. The shower curtain collapsing just when my head was sudsy. Stubbing my toe as my sandal slipped. Then my computer erased my work in a brown out and the auto back up (scheduled for every 5 minutes) decided not to kick in as it should. ARGHHH!!!!

Each time my blood pressure inched up another point or so. Every incident piled onto the other like a tower of cards wobbling in the blast of an oscillating fan.
WHAT WAS GOING ON????

My tolerance level plummeted to my toes. Perhaps it is because I have been instrumental in planning three large events and five talks coming up in the eleven weeks after coming off the roller coaster of launching a novel and jumping from book signing to book signing. When I texted a writer friend of all I had planned over the next two months, she stated she became tired just reading about it.

I finally sat with my head on my desk, tears swimming, and prayed. I prayed for Satan to quit messing with me. I prayed for the Holy Spirit to bolster me and and calm me. I prayed to the Lord to bring me His peace. I prayed for all these end-of-rope frustrations to stop. "What are you trying to tell me, Lord?"

Then, like a whisper in the ear, but from the inside out, came a voice. "I will see you through it and protect you from attacks, my child. But next time, pray to me before you take all this on."

OH! Okay. Sure. My cheeks warmed and my heart sunk. Busted.

When frustrations build, stop, breathe and pray. Above all else, pray. Perhaps our Lord allows these irritating little things to occur so we'll stop long enough to give Him our undivided attention.

DISCUSS:
How often do we overload ourselves, and then ask for strength to endure it?

How many times do we rush ahead and then reach back for Jesus' hand and try to pull Him along with us?

What makes us think we can keep running on empty and not refill through quiet God-time?

Feathered Cacophony

As I pulled into work, a strange noise hit my ears. Actually, a lot of noises. Hundreds of squawks pelted the parking lot, in unison and yet sounding individually. An enormous flock of starlings darted in and out of the trees the creek that runs alongside the church property. What struck me is that in the drumming clamor I could pick out individual bird songs.

A warmth spread over me as I thought, *that is what God hears.* All of the prayers lifted up all over the world may seem deafening, and yet He can decipher each individual one. I never have to worry if mine gets "lost" in the shuffle. Whether 15,000,000 people are praying with me or just one or two, it is heard. After all, He knows the whisperings of my heart before it even hits my brain and comes out of my mouth.

> *In the morning, Lord, you hear my voice; in the morning I lay my requests before you and wait expectantly.* Psalm 5:3

God heard His Son's sob-laden pleas in the Garden of Gethsemane, and his last words choked out on the cross. Because I believe Jesus died for me I am confident He hears my sorrowful pleas, the words that choke in my throat as well as my shouts of joys and questioning why?

Today, a feathered cacophony of birds flocking in spring reminded me that God hears. What will God's message to you be today?

DISCUSS:

Do you ever feel as if your prayers are not being heard? Why do you think that is?

Are you ever tone-deaf to God speaking to you through all the stuff going on in your thoughts? What things can you do to hear Him more often?

Wonderfully Restored

My mother had a mahogany tier table in her living room with three lion-paw legs. Three round shelves, connected by spindles, were stacked in ascending sized circles, like a wedding cake design. On it perched all of her most precious figurines. Many, like the table, were heirlooms from her mother, my grandmother. I grew up knowing about the invisible barrier around that table. Look but don't touch.

Many decades ago. I tried to teach my rambunctious two-year-old son that lesson, but when he was playing pee-pie with his grandfather, the chasing and giggles led way to disaster. He tripped and grabbed for the first thing—yep, the tier table. Down it went on top of him. The figurines catapulted into the air and, in what seemed like slo-mo, crashed to the ground, rolling, breaking, shattering. My mother and I stopped breathing.

My son lay stone-still in shock and then, as we lifted the table off of him, the trickled tears turned to wails. I carried him off to examine the bumps and bruises, my mother in tow. My mother kept whispering. "They' re just baubles. Nothing compared to my grandson."

After all was well and boo-boos kissed, we returned to the living room to survey the damage. There, sat my husband

and my dad at the dining room table with newspapers spread between them amongst tweezers, toothpicks, a magnifying glass and glue. They had separated the pieces into piles and were painstakingly gluing on fingers, noses and other porcelain body parts. It took them hours that weekend, but all but one figurine was restored.

Mom began to cry as they placed them back on the up-righted tier table. I told her. "I am so sorry. I know they have all lost their value."

Through watery eyes she whispered, "Oh, no. Now they are more precious than ever."

O God, who wonderfully created, and yet more wonderfully restored, the dignity of human nature: Grant that we may share the divine life of him who humbled himself to share our humanity, your Son Jesus Christ; who lives and reigns with you, in the unity of the Holy Spirit, one God, for ever and ever. Amen.   (Collect for the 2nd Sunday in Christmas)

DISCUSS:

What about this story resonates with you?

Are there pieces in your life you need to allow god to [painstakingly put back together?

Are there some things, like the one figurine, too broken to be restored?

Have You Mooned Anyone?

 Think back to your school days. What did you learn about the moon?

It revolved around the earth, which revolved around the sun. It doesn't have the ability on its own to create light, but the sun reflects off of it to shine upon the earth. It goes through stages. Sometimes it is full of light, while at other times it is just a slivered crescent. It makes the dark not so dark, but sometimes it even appears in the daytime, though then it is not so shiny. It has pull on the tides, and some say on human behavior. And of course, there is a man in it - or so it appears!

We Christians should be like the moon. We revolve around the Son and even though we are not of this world because our world is His Kingdom in Heaven, we are called to be His shining Light to this world. Our purpose is to reflect His love. Our Lord uses us to shine into the darkness of others' lives. But even when their lives are fine and they do not think they need our directional light, we can still be hovering as an example that God is ever-present.

As the moon has pull on the tides, we have the ability to pull others to Christ. However, let's be honest. Like the moon, we also go through phases, don't we? Sometimes we are not so full of His Light as other times. But, we will always reflect Him in our lives, even if it is just a sliver. No matter what we are going through, or how sure our faith walk is at the moment, Jesus still is evident in our lives. We can still be a beacon to others trapped in darkness.

And just as people look up and envision a man in the moon, so can they envision the Son of Man in us.

> In the same way, let your light shine before others, that they may see your good deeds and glorify your Father in heaven. Matthew 5:16

DISCUSS:

Who have you "mooned" recently?

Who has "mooned" you?

A Dung Beetle

I had to laugh. There beneath my feet was a tiny black beetle rolling a piece of deer dropping. It was easily two times larger than he (or she - how do you tell?). I thought, *I've felt like that bug.*

There have been times I had too much to bear, and wondered why. There have been times I wanted to quit because I was tired of doing what I was doing and it wasn't fun or fulfilling. There have been times I felt like my life was full of...well you get the idea.

Yet, with diligent determination, the little bug used its legs and body to push, roll and move this piece of dung over pebbles, leaves, twigs and dirt. Nothing was going to deter that little creature of God from doing what he was doing.

You may say, "Okay. I get it. But, this is a bug. It's working on instinct only. It can't think. It doesn't make decisions."
True. But what if we accepted what God has given us at the moment and just plugged along anyway? Even if it seemed

like something we'd rather not shove along at the moment, if we realize all has purpose in God's kingdom, it would help us labor on by spiritual instinct -- keep doing what God has given us to do until He says do something else, assured it is all in His plan.

Perhaps, we think too much. Perhaps we should just "do" and not over think it. That takes faith. But, if we can realize that God put us here to go through the things in our lives for a purpose, that good can come out of bad, and that He is always right beside us through the process, we'll be able to push through life with a better attitude.

> *...for it is God who works in you to will and to act in order to fulfill his good purpose.* Philippians 2:13

> *And we know that in all things God works for the good of those who love him, who have been called according to his purpose.* Romans 8:28

If I had the ear and bent close enough, I may have even heard that little beetle humming or whistling as it worked.

DISCUSS:
Are you a "doer"? How's that working for you?

Is it ever okay to quit? Why or why not?

Without the G

When a fellow author friend of mine from Canada, Linda McCutcheon, saw this sign, she could barely hold her cell phone still long enough to take the picture while she roared with laughter.

She texted me, "Why would I rent sin? I don't even want to borrow it!"

Aha—God lesson alert!! I asked her permission to use it in y blog entry because that simple sign spoke volumes to me.

Evidently someone didn't know how to spell. They left out the "G" in the word "sign". *What happens when we leave out the "G"?* Same thing. If we do not have God in the center of our lives, the "i" takes over (our selfish nature).

But with the "G" (God) in the middle, we become a sign for all who are seeking something more.

Oh, and the rent part? Well, are we not really His—as is all creation? We are just the caretakers while on this earth. We are all living in rented property until it is time to go home to Heaven. That is where our ownership is. When we forget that fact, often times sin takes over.

Finally the sign itself. Signs are supposed to point to something. We are supposed to point others to Jesus as we strive to live godly lives, but we can't do without God, can we?

DISCUSS:

When people look at you today as they go about their busyness, will they see the "g" in the middle, or not?

When are you the most likely to leave God out?

Form the V

One day as I drove down the highway, I saw geese flying in a V formation. I thought, "Wow. Odd time of year to see them. It's the middle of January. They migrate in the autumn, right?"

A chill, like a million microscopic, icy-footed ants, jumped from my heart and dashed down to my hands as they gripped the steering wheel. What I saw was an answer to prayer.

Geese fly in a V to conserve energy for the long trip. Their leader is at the point of the V. But, after a while, that leader tires of fighting the wind currents. It drops back and another takes over. The other geese support the tired one. The V formation continues, and so does their journey.

So should be the same for us Christians, no matter our ministry. I will admit it. I'm tired— emotionally, physically and a bit spiritually. I've been flapping my wings like mad but felt as if I made little progress. It showed in the darkening circles under my eyes.

Through these geese, God revealed to me it is time for me to drop back and let someone else take over. "But Lord," I asked. "My terms as president is not over for five months in one organization, and a year in another. There is still a long journey ahead."

Suddenly, one of the geese flew to the front of the V. I watched as the leader dropped back a pace or two, but not to the end of the line. It positioned itself near the front, just behind a place or two. I had my answer.

Oh, yeah, My Lord is the one who should take over at the tip of the V. He's the one who never tires, controls the wind, and always knows the direction we are going. Somewhere along the way, I'd lost sight of that fact. I'd been flapping so hard, my head was downcast against the winds—my eyes squeezed tight in determination, my teeth clamped together as I trudged on. No wonder I've been so tense... and exhausted. God made me realize (again) that I am not flying this journey alone. He's been flying there with me the whole time.

Yes, my soul, find rest in God; my hope comes from him. Psalm 62:5

DISCUSS:
Where in your life do you need to drop back and let God lead a while?

Are you willing to let someone else be ahead of you?

Hands and Feet

Did you know our thickest layers of skin are on our hands and feet?

Evolutionists state it is because we once walked on all fours. But, I think it is by God's design because He wants us to be Christ's hands and feet on the earth until He returns for His own.

Sometimes, in order to do that, you need to become pretty thick-skinned, while still remaining softhearted on the inside. You need to put yourself aside and become callous to comments, knowing that you are all about doing the Lord's work, not the feeding of your own ego.
Jesus told his disciples, and He tells us,

> *"If the world hates you, keep in mind that it hated me first. If you belonged to the world, it would love you as its own. As it is, you do not belong to the world, but I have chosen you out of the world. That is why the world hates you."* John 15:18-19

Yet He loved us all enough to stretch out His hands and feet upon the cross.

Your hands and feet are meant to be thick and calloused if they are constantly doing His work. So labor on, Christian. Toughen-up and be willing stretch them out for His sake, and for the sake of the lost.

DISCUSS:

Has another believer ever treated you poorly? What did you do about it?

Are you one to ruminate on what others think of you or perhaps what you overheard someone say about you? Or does it not affect you in the least?

Have you ever felt you were not capable of being God's hands and feet? What happened? What did you learn from the experience?

Impossible Pie

I spoke at women's breakfast recently. One of the dishes they served was the Impossible Pie.

What is incredible is that you pour all the ingredients into a pie pan, shove it in the

oven, and as if by magic, the layers separate as it cooks into a tasty quiche-like meal. It comes out perfectly - crust on bottom, cheese on top and the eggs and other ingredients fluffed up in the center. Seems impossible.

You know this is going to turn into a devotional—so here goes.

Our lives can be like the impossible pie. All the things that are happening to us can be mixed up and shuffled together. We just can't see it all coming together in a right way. But with God in control, all things will come together and turn out in perfect order.

When we follow God's instructions, everything is perfectly measured, even though we think, *Now, how in the world can that turn into something good? That's not how I'd do it.*

God's fiery furnace will bring it all together in a wonderful way. We just need to trust in that fact.

If you feel the heat turning up a bit in your life, take to heart what Peter wrote in his first letter.

> *"Dear friends, do not be surprised at the fiery ordeal that has come on you to test you, as though something strange were happening to you."*
> 1Peter 4:12

Let God work in your life and slowly, things will get in order. The end result will be Incredible, even though you thought it impossible at first.

DISCUSS:

Have you ever obediently done something even though you were convinced it would not turn out? Did it?

Why do you think we often don't see things come together until after the fact?

Saved a Place

It still crawls into the back of my emotions and stings me. Memories loom into my brain of being the last person to be picked on the team, or being shunned from the cafeteria table of giggling girls as I slid off to a corner to eat alone. Being the brunt of cruel jokes in junior high because I was smart, and the subject of gossip in the college dorm because I was a Christian who wouldn't sleep around or drink. Never fitting in.

I was at a women's conference manning a table for Women at Risk- the missionaries for women rescued from human trafficking (see Help a Woman Find God tab). We were in a large meeting hall where rounds tables had been set for lunch. Everyone flowed in form the meeting, chatting and laughing. As I helped a few ladies buy jewelry and handbags made by the rescued women, I saw the tables were filling up. Women came up to them and said, "Come on. I saved you a place." They each scurried off giggling, showing their friends what they had purchased.

The other women began to settle into their places to listen to the speaker as they ate. The tables filled quickly. I waited until the last person left my vendor booth before I went to get my lunch. I was fully prepared eat at my booth—alone again.

Then, a woman whom I hadn't seen in a while came up to me. "We have saved you a place. Won't you please sit with us?" Those old feelings dispelled like a popped water balloon. When I got to the table, it was all smiles and "so good to see you", "glad you joined us" responses.

Jesus told His disciples, and He tells us today, that He is preparing a place for us in Heaven. Each believer who confesses His name is accepted at the table of The Lamb. One day we will all be allowed to feast on His presence for eternity.

At that meeting, I saw a glimpse of how glorious that will be. As a woman of God, I am accepted by my sisters in Christ. So are you. We are all foreigners in a strange land bound by a love the world cannot understand. There is a place for you right here beside us. Won't you come join us?

DISCUSS:

How does this story resonate with you?

What old memories and hurts are you carrying around that you need to finally drop now that you know Christ loves and forgives you?

Notes, Reflections: